Dominoes

THE LOST WORLD

OXFORD

OXFORD
UNIVERSITY PRESS

Great Clarendon Street, Oxford OX2 6DP

Oxford University Press is a department of the University of Oxford.
It furthers the University's objective of excellence in research, scholarship,
and education by publishing worldwide in

Oxford New York

Auckland Cape Town Dar es Salaam Hong Kong Karachi
Kuala Lumpur Madrid Melbourne Mexico City Nairobi
New Delhi Shanghai Taipei Toronto

With offices in

Argentina Austria Brazil Chile Czech Republic France Greece
Guatemala Hungary Italy Japan Poland Portugal Singapore
South Korea Switzerland Thailand Turkey Ukraine Vietnam

OXFORD and OXFORD ENGLISH are registered trade marks of
Oxford University Press in the UK and in certain other countries

First published 2002
2011 2010 2009 2008 2007
10 9 8

A complete recording of this Dominoes edition of *The Lost World*
is available on cassette ISBN 978 0 19 424361 2

ISBN 978 0 19 424347 6

Printed in Hong Kong

ACKNOWLEDGEMENTS

The publisher would like to thank the following for permission to use their copyright material:
Dover Publications (p iv); The Natural History Museum, London (p 56); Christopher Tomlin (pp 57, 58)
All other illustrations are by: Anders Westerberg of Stockholm Illustration

Dominoes

SERIES EDITORS: BILL BOWLER AND SUE PARMINTER

THE LOST WORLD

SIR ARTHUR CONAN DOYLE

Text adaptation by Susan Kingsley

Illustrated by Anders Westerberg

LEVEL TWO ■ 700 HEADWORDS

Sir Arthur Conan Doyle (1859–1930), born in Edinburgh, Scotland, is best known for his tales of Sherlock Holmes, the detective, though he also wrote many science fiction stories. He started writing after working as a doctor, and soon became one of the world's best known authors. His story about the detective Sherlock Holmes, *The Blue Diamond*, is also available as a Domino.

OXFORD

BEFORE READING

1 What do you know about dinosaurs and other animals of their time? Fill in the table.

	 Triceratops	 Stegosaurus	 Pterodactyl	 Tyrannosaurus Rex
When did it live?	67–75 million years ago (Cretaceous period)			
Where did it live?	in what is now North America			
What did it look like?	It had three horns, a bit like today's rhinoceros			
How heavy was it?	4.8 tonnes			
How big was it?	9 metres long			
What did it eat?	plants			
How did it move?	in groups			

2 Which films or TV programmes have you seen with dinosaurs in them?

CHAPTER 1
WHERE ARE THESE GREAT ADVENTURES?

How beautiful she was! Her large, soft eyes, her long, dark hair, her sweet smile – Gladys Hungerton was made for love. We were friends, good friends, but nothing more. We sat, silently, by the window in her father's house, and Gladys seemed so beautiful, but so far away. Tonight, I decided, tonight I would ask her. Suddenly, she turned to me, and said:

'I have a **feeling** that you're going to ask me to marry you, Ned. Please don't.'

feeling something that you feel inside yourself

'How did you know?' I asked, very surprised.

'Women always know,' she replied. 'But don't you think that things are nicer as they are? We're good friends, we can talk so openly and so easily together.'

'But I want more than that, Gladys. I want to hold you in my arms, I want . . . Oh, Gladys, why can't you love me?'

'Because I love another man,' she replied.

Gladys saw the surprise on my face.

'Oh, I've never met him,' she laughed, and explained. 'He's just an **idea** in my head.'

'Tell me about him,' I said.

'Well, he possibly has your face, but . . .'

'But . . . what?' I asked. 'Tell me, Gladys, just tell me what you want. I can change!'

'He is a harder man than you. He is a man who does **brave** things, and has strange adventures. He is a man who can look at death in the face, and is not afraid.'

'But we can't all have adventures,' I said. 'And where are these great adventures? I've never found one.'

'They are all around us. But it is only the great men who see them. And I know that if I marry, I want to marry a famous man.'

'And why not?' I said, suddenly, and jumped to my feet. 'Yes, I'll do something great in the world. I will! And, when I've done it—'

Gladys put a soft hand over my mouth.

'Don't say another word. You're already half an hour late for the office. One day, when you've won your place in the world, we'll talk about it again.'

That was how it all began. As I waited for my bus in the dark, rainy London streets, something was burning inside me. I was twenty-three, an unimportant young **reporter** on the *Daily Gazette* newspaper, but I felt inside me the hot fire of first love. Tonight, I was sure, I would find something that would change my life. I would find a great thing to do, a brave adventure somewhere out in the world, and I would win my Gladys's love.

idea a plan or a new thought

brave not afraid of doing dangerous things

reporter a person who writes for a newspaper

So, that cold November evening, I arrived at the office of the *Gazette* with my head full of these ideas. Mr McArdle, the news **editor**, was at his desk. I always liked old McArdle, and I hoped that he liked me.

'I hear that you are doing very well, Mr Malone,' he said, in his kind Scottish voice. 'You have written some very good pieces for us.'

'Thank you,' I answered.

'Now, how can I help you?'

'**Sir**, I . . . I have something to ask you. Do you think that you could possibly send me somewhere with a lot of adventure and danger? I'll try to write something good for the *Gazette*, I really will.'

'Were you thinking of anywhere special?'

'Not really. But somewhere very difficult. I want something really hard.'

editor a person who decides which stories must go in a newspaper

sir when you are speaking to a man that you do not know well, or who is more important than you, you call him this

professor an important teacher at a university

zoologist a person who studies animals

liar a person who says things that are not true

throw to push something or somebody quickly through the air with your hands

'Oh dear me, Mr Malone. That's very brave of you,' replied McArdle. 'Do you really want to lose your life so young?'

'No, I want to find out what my life really means.'

'Mr Malone, the days of young reporters going on dangerous adventures are past, I'm afraid. These days editors only give jobs like that to famous reporters,' he said. But then a sudden smile came to his face. 'Wait a minute! I have an idea. Why don't you go and see **Professor** Challenger?'

'Professor Challenger! The famous **zoologist**!' was my surprised reply. 'Didn't he break the arm of that reporter from *The Times*?'

'Yes, but I'm hoping that you'll have better luck. And you said that you wanted danger, didn't you? Here are some notes for you to begin with.'

He gave me a paper and I read it quickly.

Professor George Edward Challenger

Born: **1863, Scotland**
Spent school and student days in Edinburgh

Job: **Zoologist.**
Winner of Crayston Cup for his work as a zoologist (London 1892-3)
Has very different ideas from other zoologists

Likes: **Mountain climbing, walking**

Address: **Enmore Park, London**

'But, sir,' I said to McArdle, putting the paper in my pocket. 'I don't understand. Why do I need to talk to this man? What has he done?'

McArdle's round, red face looked up from his newspaper.

'He spent a year alone, in a place somewhere in South America. No one knows where it was. He came back to London last year, and he said one or two things about his travels, but then people started asking questions and he stopped talking so freely. Either something wonderful happened there – or the man's a **liar**. Most people think he's a liar. So now he hits anybody who asks him questions, and he **throws** reporters downstairs. That's your man, Mr Malone. Go and see what you think of him.'

And that was the end of the conversation. I went out, and for a long time I looked into the brown, cloudy waters of the River Thames, looking for ideas. Then, suddenly I knew what to do. I went at once to see Tarp Henry, a **scientist**, and an old friend of mine.

'Challenger?' said Henry. 'He was the man who came back from South America with that impossible story. He said that he **discovered** some strange animals there. There were even some photographs, but nobody **believes** that they're real.'

Tarp Henry showed me some of Challenger's books, and I opened the largest one. After a long time, I found a few words which I could nearly understand. I wrote them on a paper, and began my letter.

Dear Professor Challenger,

I am a young zoologist who has always been greatly interested in your works—

'You liar!' laughed Henry.

I went on writing, asking if the great Professor would kindly agree to see me on Wednesday, to talk about some of the ideas in his book.

'He's a dangerous man,' said Henry, reading my letter. 'But, luckily for you, I don't think that he'll answer this.'

My friend was wrong. At eleven o'clock that Wednesday morning I was knocking on the front door of Challenger's fine house, with a letter from the Professor in my hand.

scientist a person who studies the natural world

discover to find something new or important

believe to feel sure that something is true

READING CHECK

Are these sentences true or false? Tick the boxes.

		T	F
a	Gladys wants to marry Malone soon.	☐	✔
b	Malone works for Mr McArdle, a Canadian newspaper man.	☐	☐
c	McArdle sends Malone to speak to George Edward Challenger.	☐	☐
d	Challenger spent a year in South America.	☐	☐
e	Challenger is a very friendly man.	☐	☐
f	Malone speaks to his friend Tarp Henry about Challenger.	☐	☐
g	Tarp Henry says Challenger found strange animals in South America.	☐	☐
h	Challenger asks Malone to come to his house.	☐	☐

WORD WORK

1 Use these words to complete the sentences.

reporter
editor
professor
zoologist
~~scientist~~
liar

a Are you an artist or a scientist?
Oh, no! I'm not an artist! I'm a .... I love studying animals! b
What do you do?
c I'm a newspaper .... I choose the pieces that go in *The Times*.
Really? d I'm a .... Can I send you some of my writing?
I see!
e I'm a .... at Oxford University. I teach the students there all about modern music.
f My boyfriend's a .... He's always telling people things which aren't true.

2 Find the words to complete the sentences about the story.

a Gladys has an i dea that Malone wants to marry her.

b She says that she wants to marry a b _ _ _ _ man.

c Malone has the f _ _ _ _ _ _ that he must win Gladys's love.

d People say that Challenger visited a 'l _ _ _ world' in South America.

e They say that he d _ _ _ _ _ _ _ _ _ strange animals there.

f Many people don't b _ _ _ _ _ _ Challenger's stories.

g When people from the newspapers visit Challenger, he likes to t _ _ _ _ them downstairs.

GUESS WHAT

What happens in the next chapter? Tick four boxes.

- **a** Malone meets Challenger. ☐
- **b** Challenger thinks that Malone is a young scientist. ☐
- **c** Challenger is very friendly. ☐
- **d** Challenger throws Malone downstairs. ☐
- **e** Malone leaves Challenger's house and never sees him again. ☐
- **f** Challenger shows Malone something interesting. ☐
- **g** Malone wants to meet Challenger again. ☐

CHAPTER 2
IT'S JUST THE BIGGEST THING IN THE WORLD

When I stood face to face with the Professor at his home in Enmore Park I could not believe what I saw. He had the most **enormous** head that I have ever seen, a very big body, and great hairy hands. His face was an angry red colour, and his great **beard** was blue-black. He sat and looked at me with eyes of a very deep grey.

enormous very big

beard the hair on a man's face

attack to start fighting

'Well?' he said, at last.

I tried to talk like a scientist, but the Professor did not believe me for a minute.

'You dirty little reporter! Did you really think that you could be as clever as the great G.E. Challenger?'

Challenger jumped to his feet, and I was surprised to see that he was only a short man. Then he **attacked** me. His great body was on top of me, and then I was on top of him, and my mouth was full of his beard. Our bodies went flying out of the room, and we suddenly found ourselves in the street. A policeman stood beside us, with a little book in his hand.

'What's all this, then?' he asked, looking at the Professor. 'You were in trouble for the same thing last month, weren't you?' He opened his book and started to write notes in it.

'No, please don't,' I said. 'This time I began it, I'm afraid. He didn't mean to hurt me.'

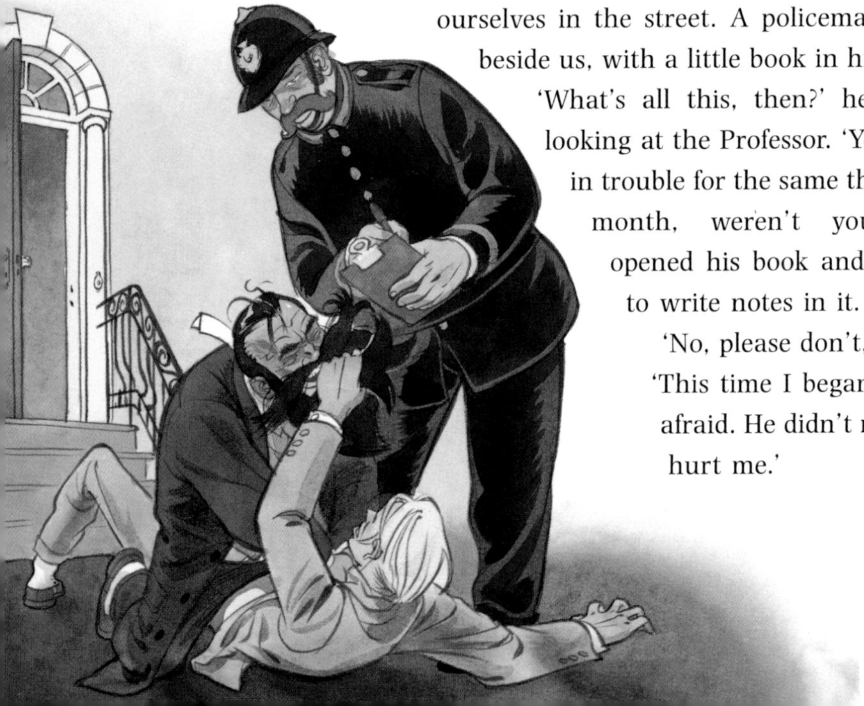

The policeman stopped writing and told the crowd of people in the street to go away. The Professor looked at me, with a small smile in his deep grey eyes.

'Come in! I've not finished with you yet.'

A little afraid, I followed him into the house. We went back into his room, where he showed me a comfortable chair.

'Now, listen carefully,' he began. 'I usually have no time for people from the newspapers. But your words to that policeman showed me that you are, perhaps, a little better than the rest of them. That is why I brought you back.

'Now, you know that I made a journey to South America two years ago. Very few white people have visited the small rivers which run into the great Amazon River.

'One night I was in a village deep in the **forest**. The **Indians** there took me to see a very ill white man in one of their homes. When I arrived, he was already dead. Beside him lay a bag. When I opened it, I saw the name *Maple White*, and an address in America. I also found something else. It was this book of his **drawings**. Look at it closely.'

He stopped, took an old, dirty, drawing book from his desk and gave it to me. There were drawings of Indians, and a picture of a white man, with the words *Jimmy Colver on the boat* below it. The other drawings were of animals and birds.

'I see nothing unusual here,' I said, and I turned the pages.

The next drawing interested me more. It showed some very high, dark red **cliffs**. They lay across the page, like a great red wall, with green trees all along the top. One great, tall **rock** stood alone next to the cliffs.

'Now . . . look at the last page,' said the Professor, smiling.

I turned the page, and nearly screamed. I was looking at a wild, strange animal. It had a small head, short legs, and an enormous blue-grey body, perhaps nine metres long.

'Now look at this,' he said, and he showed me a **bone**. It was about fifteen centimetres long, with some dry skin at

forest a place with a lot of trees

Indian a person who lived in America before white people arrived

drawing a picture made with a pen or pencil

cliff a high natural wall

rock a very big stone

bone a hard white thing inside an animal's body

one end. 'I found it in the American's bag. The same bone in a man's body is like this,' he went on, and he showed me a bone about one centimetre long. 'So you can see it came from a very large animal. And the skin on the end tells you that the bone is not very old. Well, what do you think? What is it?'

'I'm afraid that I've no idea,' I replied.

'Then I'll tell you, young man. This bone belongs to a **dinosaur**. The drawing is of a dinosaur too. Scientists think that they all died millions of years ago, but I can tell you that some dinosaurs are still alive today. So, what do you say now?'

'I'm deeply interested,' I said.

Next, the Professor showed me a large, very dark photograph. I looked at it closely. I could see an enormous wall of cliffs; beside them stood a tall, single rock, with a great tree on top.

'I think it's the same place as the drawing,' I said.

'It is. I found things from Maple White's **camp** there. Now, look at that tree. Can you see something there?'

'A large bird?' I said.

'Not a bird,' replied Challenger. 'Would you like to see a piece of its wing?'

The Professor opened a box, and took out a long bone with some grey skin on it. Then he opened a book on his desk, and showed me a picture of a strange flying animal.

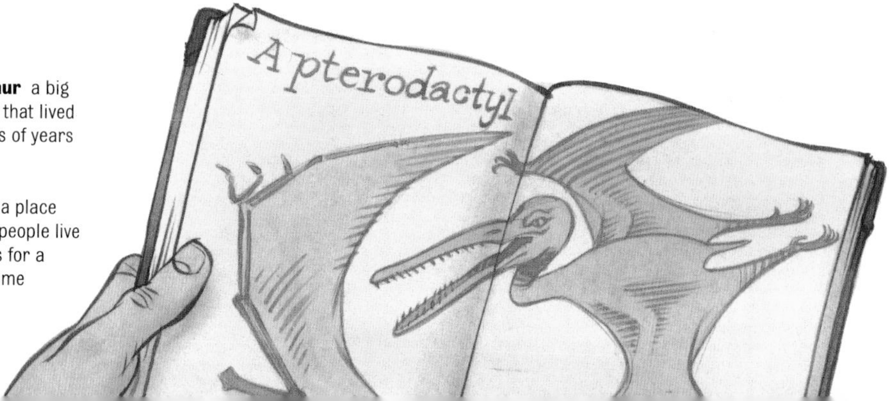

dinosaur a big animal that lived millions of years ago

camp a place where people live in tents for a short time

'This is a picture of the **pterodactyl**,' he said, 'and that is a drawing of the bones in a pterodactyl's wing.'

I looked at the book, and at the bone. And I was sure it was all true!

'Professor, this is just the biggest thing in the world! You're a great scientist who has found a lost world.'

The Professor sat back in his chair, with a great, warm smile on his face.

'And did you see any more living things there, sir?' I asked.

'No. I heard many strange sounds from the top of the cliffs, but I could not find a way to climb up there.'

'But how did the animals get there?'

'They have been there for a long time,' replied Challenger. 'The rest of the world changed and all the dinosaurs died. But life on those cliffs has stayed the same for millions of years.'

'Professor, this is wonderful news! You must tell the world about it,' I said.

'I have tried, but nobody believed me. Stupid people!' replied the Professor. 'But tonight I'll try again. At eight-thirty tonight there is a **meeting** at the **Zoological Institute**. They have asked me to thank the speaker, Mr Waldron, at the end of the meeting. While I'm doing that, I'll say one or two interesting things, and perhaps people will want to learn more. If I tell my story quietly and carefully, perhaps they'll listen to me. Will you come? I'd like to have somebody in the room who is on my side – even somebody who knows as little as you do.'

With a large, kind smile, he gave me a ticket from his desk.

'You will not put a word of this in your newspaper. Do you understand? Now, goodbye. You have already taken too much of my important time today. I'll see you at eight-thirty.'

TALK
AT THE
ZOOLOGICAL INSTITUTE
8.30 p.m.
Wednesday 17th November
Mr Waldron will speak about the history of the world. Professor Challenger will finish the evening with a few words of thanks.

pterodactyl /ˌterəˈdæktɪl/ a flying animal that lived millions of years ago

meeting when a number of people come together to talk about something important

Zoological Institute a place where zoologists meet to talk about their work and studies

READING CHECK

Put these sentences in the correct order. Number them 1-9.

a ☐ A policeman comes to speak to Challenger.

b ☐ Challenger becomes friendly and asks Malone to go into his house.

c ☐ Challenger and Malone fight in the street.

d ☐ Challenger shows some other strange things to Malone.

e ☐ Challenger gives Maple White's book to Malone.

f [1] Challenger throws Malone out of his house.

g ☐ Malone tells the policeman that Challenger didn't start the fight.

h ☐ Challenger asks Malone to come and hear a talk that evening.

i ☐ Malone looks at the pictures in Maple White's book.

WORD WORK

1 These words don't match the pictures. Correct them.

a ~~rock~~ dinosaur

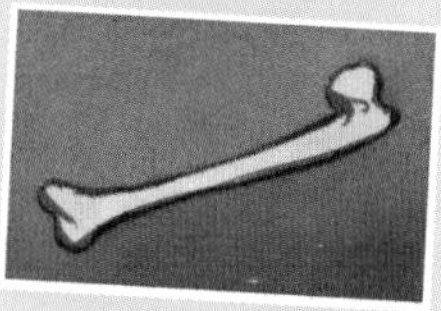

b beard ……………………

c pterodactyl ……………………

d dinosaur ……………………

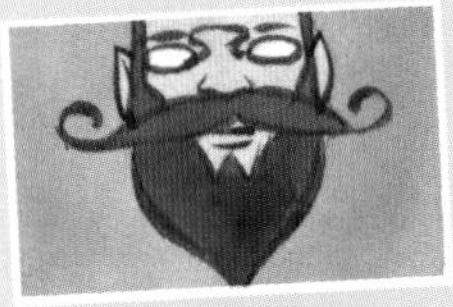

e forest ……………………

f bone ……………………

g camp ……………………

h cliff ……………………

2 Use the words in the dinosaur to complete the sentences.

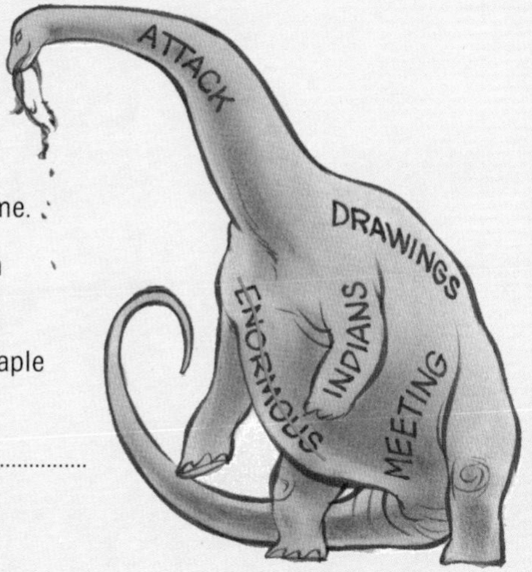

a Challenger has an ...enormous... head.

b I wouldn't like a dinosaur to .... me.

c There are some interesting .... in Maple White's book.

d Amazon .... took Challenger to Maple White when he was dying.

e Challenger asks Malone to come to a .... at the Zoological Institute.

GUESS WHAT

Who goes to the meeting at the Zoological Institute? Tick three boxes.

a ☐ McArdle

b ☐ Gladys

c ☐ Challenger

d ☐ Malone

e ☐ Tarp Henry

f ☐ A policeman

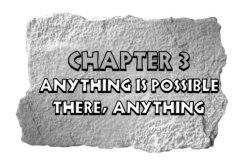

CHAPTER 3
ANYTHING IS POSSIBLE THERE, ANYTHING

'My dear friend, I don't believe a word of what the man says,' said Tarp Henry, while we were having dinner together that night.

'But what about the drawing of the dinosaur?' I asked.

'Challenger drew it himself,' answered Henry.

'And the bones?'

'He took them from his dinner plate,' was Henry's reply.

I began to worry. Perhaps Tarp Henry was right? Maybe Challenger was just a good liar.

'Will you come to the meeting?' I asked.

'There aren't many people in London who like Challenger, you know. What if there's trouble?'

Henry thought for a while, but at last he agreed to come.

The great room at the Zoological Institute was already full when we arrived. There were old men and young men, professors with white beards, and noisy, laughing students. One by one, the scientists took their seats at the long table at the front of the room, and the students called something to each of them. Their loudest shouts were for Challenger.

When everyone was quiet, the speaker began his talk. Mr Waldron spoke of the beginnings of life on **Earth**. He talked of the great dinosaurs, and said:

'Luckily, these terrible animals were all dead a long time before men arrived in the world.'

'Question!' **roared** a voice from the front table.

Mr Waldron waited a while, then he said the same words again, more slowly and loudly.

'Question!' roared the voice once more.

The speaker looked round, and saw Challenger. He was sitting back, with his eyes closed, and a large smile on his face.

Earth the world we live on

roar to make a loud noise like a big animal

'I see!' said Mr Waldron. 'It is my friend Professor Challenger.'

The students all laughed, and the speaker went on. But every time that Mr Waldron spoke about dinosaurs, the Professor roared 'Question!' and the crowd laughed more and more loudly. Mr Waldron became uncomfortable and angry, and his talk soon ended. Challenger then stood up.

'I'd like to thank the speaker for his interesting little talk. Mr Waldron believes that dinosaurs all died millions of years ago. This is because he has never seen one. But I know that these animals are still here with us today. How do I know? I know because I have visited their secret places. I know because I have seen them.'

There was much shouting and laughing from the crowd, and a voice called 'Liar!'

'Who said that?' roared Challenger, his eyes on fire. 'It is the same for all great discoverers. We try to tell people about wonderful things, and they believe nothing. Stupid people!'

The crowd went wild. They jumped to their feet, and shouted. But then the Professor held up his two great hands, and the room slowly became quiet again. Everybody was listening.

'I have discovered a lost world. Will any of you go to find out if my words are true or not?'

Professor Summerlee stood up from the crowd. He was a tall, thin, grey, unsmiling man.

'You say that you have seen dinosaurs. But you do not tell us where these animals are, or how we can find them,' he said in his cold, dry voice.

'I'll tell you if you agree to come to South America with me to see the dinosaurs for

yourself. Will you do that?'

'Yes, I will,' came Summerlee's reply.

The crowd **cheered**.

'Very well. But it will be a difficult and dangerous journey, so we need a younger man with us. Who will go with us?' asked Challenger, looking into the crowd.

There are important times in every man's life which change that man's world for ever. Suddenly I understood – this was what Gladys meant. A second later, I was on my feet, with Tarp Henry pulling at my coat.

'Sit down, Malone! Don't be so stupid,' he was saying to me.

At the same time, a few seats in front of me, a tall thin man with dark red hair was also standing up.

'I'll go,' I said.

'Name! Name!' shouted the crowd.

'My name is Malone. I'm a reporter from the *Daily Gazette.*'

'And I'm Lord John Roxton,' said the tall man with the red hair. 'I've already been up the Amazon. I know it well.'

So this was Lord John Roxton, the famous traveller and sportsman, I thought.

'Very well. Both these men will travel with Professor Summerlee and myself,' said Challenger.

cheer to shout to show that you are pleased

Then the doors opened and the noisy crowd pushed out into the street, taking me with them. I found myself alone under the silver street lights, thinking about Gladys and the adventures that were waiting for me. Suddenly a hand touched my arm. I turned, and saw the smiling face of Lord John.

'Mr Malone, will you come over to my place? I'd like to talk to you.'

I followed Lord John to his flat. On the walls there were many things from his sporting days, and animal heads and skins from his many travels. We sat down, and Lord John opened a bottle of good wine. He was tall, and very strong, with a thin face, and skin that was red from years outside in the sun and wind. His eyes were a strange light blue colour, like the **clear** water of a mountain **lake**.

'We need to get ready,' he said. 'Now, you'll need a gun.'

He opened a tall cupboard made of dark wood, took out a beautiful brown and silver **rifle** from it and gave it to me.

'On my last trip to South America I helped some Indian **slaves** in Peru,' he said. 'I fought against the **slave-drivers** there with this gun. Do you see these cuts on it? Every time I killed a slave-driver I made a cut with a knife. This big cut here is for Pedro Lopez, the worst of them. I shot him on the Putomayo River three years ago.'

Then Lord John asked, 'What do you know about Challenger?'

I told him about my morning with the Professor.

'I believe that every word of his story is true,' said Lord John. 'I know South America very well. It's the biggest, wildest, and most beautiful place in the world. Anything is possible there – anything. And if there is something new out there, perhaps we'll be the men who discover it. Why not?'

A week later, I said goodbye to grey, rainy England, and got on a ship that was sailing across the great Atlantic Ocean. Who knows what we will find on the other side?

clear you can see it, or see through it easily

lake a large piece of water with land around it

rifle a long gun

slave a person who must work for no money

slave-driver someone who hits slaves if they do not work enough

READING CHECK

Match the first and second parts of these sentences.

a	Tarp Henry . . .	**1**	. . . to go with Challenger, Malone, and Summerlee.
b	Mr Waldron thinks . . .	**2**	. . . to his flat.
c	Professor Challenger thinks . . .	**3**	. . . tells Malone that Challenger's stories about South America aren't true.
d	Professor Summerlee . . .	**4**	. . . leave for South America a week later.
e	Malone says . . .	**5**	. . . wants to know where Challenger's dinosaurs are.
f	Lord John Roxton decides . . .	**6**	. . . that there are some dinosaurs alive today.
g	Roxton asks Malone to go . . .	**7**	. . . that he will go with Professor Summerlee to South America.
h	Challenger, Summerlee, Roxton, and Malone . . .	**8**	. . . that all dinosaurs were dead when men arrived in the world.

WORD WORK

Correct the mistakes in these sentences.

a Everyone **cheesed** at the end of the meeting. cheered

b Roxton gave Malone a beautiful **raffle**. ....

c He told Malone about the time he helped Indian **staves** in Peru. ....

d Roxton's eyes were a **clean** blue colour. ....

e Titicaca is the name of a large **lane** which is half in Peru and half in Bolivia. ....

f There are some places on the **early** that few people have visited. ....

g When big animals **boar**, other animals hear and feel afraid. ....

GUESS WHAT

What happens in the next chapter? Tick the boxes.

1 They travel to the Amazon by . . .

2

. . . watch them.

3 They arrive at a place with . . .

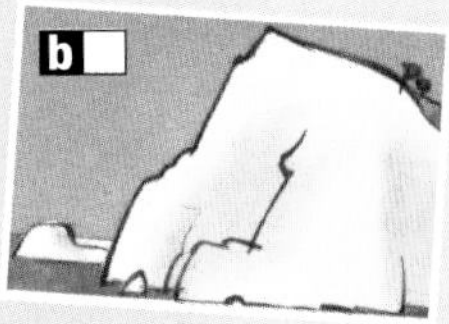

4 They find . . .

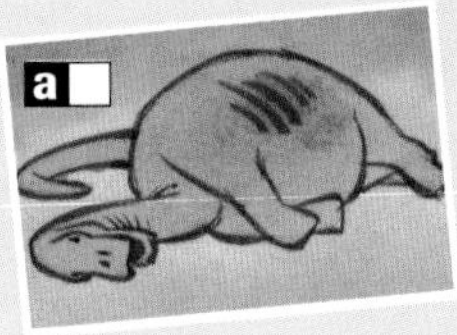

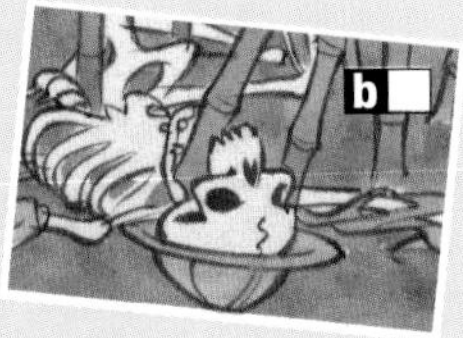

5 Someone tries to kill them with . . .

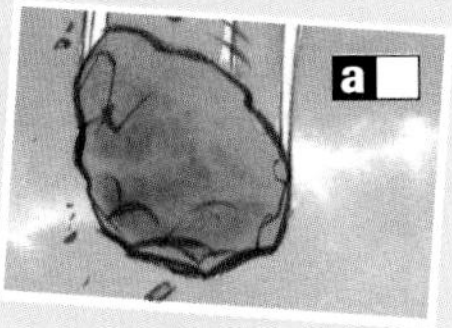

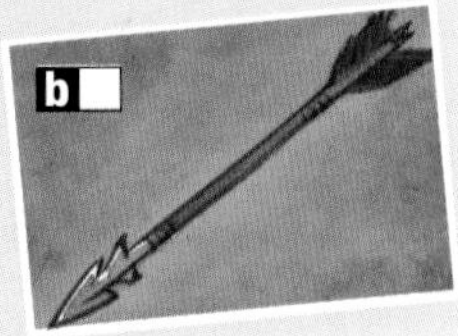

CHAPTER 4
A DOOR INTO A SECRET WORLD

After a comfortable crossing, we arrived in Brazil, and took a river boat to the town of Manaos. From here we began our journey deep into the Amazon forest – Lord John and myself, and the two professors, who **argued** about everything, like two children. We also had with us five Indians, and a fine, strong **servant** called Zambo. Also in our group were Gomez and Manuel, two men from Peru who knew about the Amazon, and who were happy to help us with our travels.

We sailed up the Amazon in two small boats. We made sure that the professors were in different boats, and at first the journey went well. For two days we saw no other living thing. Then on the third day we heard a strange, deep sound all around us. Our Indians stopped suddenly, very afraid.

'What is it?' I asked.

'Indian **drums**, sir,' said Gomez. 'The Amazon Indians are watching us.'

All that day the drums followed us. That night when we made our camp, we made ourselves ready for a possible attack. But no attack came, and the next day we sailed on. The drums became quieter and quieter, and then we heard them no more.

Late that morning, Challenger suddenly shouted, 'Aha! There it is!' and **pointed** to a strange, thin tree beside the river. 'I used that tree to find my way last time. Half a mile from here the dark green **plants** of the forest floor will stop on one side of the river, and for a short while we'll see light green river plants. That is the door into a secret world.'

Challenger was right. We found the place, pushed through the river plants, and sailed into a **tunnel** of soft, green sunlight. The tall trees met at the top, making a green **roof** high above us. Gold sunlight fell softly down through the trees,

argue to talk angrily with someone when you do not agree with them

servant a person who works for someone rich

drum a musical instrument that you hit

point to show where something is with your finger

plant a small green thing, with leaves and, sometimes with flowers

tunnel a long hole which goes under or through something

roof the top part of something

bringing strange, beautiful colours to the quiet waters below.

We sailed silently along a river that was as still as glass and bright as **diamonds**. Animal life was all around us, too. Bright red and blue birds flew over our heads, and small animals watched us, unafraid, from between the trees. The clear water was alive with fish, large and small, and of every colour. But we did not see or hear a single man.

After three days we hid our boats, and continued on foot. Challenger and Summerlee were still arguing about everything. Then we discovered that the professors both had the same enemy, a zoologist called Dr Illingworth. We found that when we dropped the name of this man into the conversation, our fighting professors soon became friends again.

Our new road took us out of the green tunnel, and up a hillside, where the forest became thinner. Then we found a group of four large, blackened stones on the ground. It was Challenger's campfire from his last journey. We went up and up, and the ground became more rocky. After nine days we came out of the trees, pushed through a forest of **bamboo**, and came into open, hilly ground. We climbed the first hill, and Challenger suddenly stopped, and pointed to the right.

About a mile away, we saw something very large and grey. It opened a pair of great wings, and flew slowly into some trees.

'Look, Summerlee!' shouted Challenger. 'A pterodactyl!'

'A ptero-nothing!' said Summerlee, with a thin, cold smile on his face. 'It was a big bird!'

diamond a hard, bright, very expensive stone that usually has no colour

bamboo a plant with very long, thin, hard sticks

Challenger's great face went purple, but he said nothing, and we went on with our journey. After a short while I heard Lord John's quiet voice in my ear.

'I saw it well,' he said. 'I've no idea what it was. But I've seen many birds in my life, and I'm sure that wasn't a bird.'

Later that day we climbed a second hill and there, at last, we saw our journey's end. In front of us stood a great wall of high, red cliffs – the cliffs of Maple White's drawing.

That night we made our camp immediately under the cliffs. Close to us stood the high, **pinnacle** of rock, with its one great tree on top. Both the cliff and the pinnacle were about two hundred metres high. It was a wild and lonely place, and we could clearly never climb up to the **plateau** from there. So when morning came, we decided to walk along the bottom of the cliffs, looking for a way up.

The ground was rocky, and our journey was slow and difficult. But then we found something which brought us hope. It was an old camp, with some empty bottles, food **tins**, and an old American newspaper.

'Look here!' said Lord John, pointing at a tree beside the camp. 'Somebody's drawn a white **arrow** on this.'

'Well then, we must follow it,' said Challenger.

We followed the arrow, but it took us to something terrible. Just below the cliff, there was a high wall of bamboo. Many of its sticks were seven metres high, with **sharp** tops. Suddenly I saw something white, lying inside the bamboo wall. I looked closely, and saw the dry bones of a man's body. A few **ragged** clothes, an expensive watch, and a silver pen lay beside the bones. On the watch was the name of a New York shop, and on the silver pen were the letters *JC*.

'An American called James Colver travelled with Maple White,' said Challenger. 'Look at the letters on the pen. These are Colver's bones, there's no question about it.'

pinnacle a very high, thin rock

plateau a large, hill with a flat top

tin a round metal box

arrow this points to where something is

sharp that can cut or make holes like a knife

ragged very old and in pieces (of clothes)

'And I think I can tell you how he met his death,' said Lord John. 'He fell from the cliffs – or someone threw him.'

I felt sure that Lord John was right. We all looked up at the cliffs. Dark ideas came into our heads about this strange place, and its terrible dangers.

For three long days, we walked slowly around the bottom of the cliffs, but we found no break in the great wall of rock. Then on the fourth day, we saw something which gave us new hope. It was another arrow. We left the Indians to make our camp while the rest of us followed the arrow. At first we found nothing. But then Lord John's quick eyes saw it – a dark circle on the face of the rock. It was the mouth of a **cave**. We climbed up to the cave, and there we found a third arrow. Gomez and Manuel stayed at the mouth of the cave, while we made our way into the black hole. So this was how Maple White got up to the plateau!

We followed the dark tunnel for about fifty metres, climbing all the time. But then, we met a wall of broken rocks.

'The roof has fallen in!' called Lord John.

We could go no further. Unhappily, we turned round, and made our way back to our camp, leaving Gomez and Manuel still up at the mouth of the cave.

We arrived at our camp sad and tired. Then suddenly an enormous rock fell from above, nearly killing us all.

'We saw it fly past us, sir. It came from up there,' called Gomez, pointing at the cliff-top.

We looked up, but saw nothing. But one thing was sure – someone, or something up there was trying to kill us.

cave a large hole in the side of a mountain

activities

READING CHECK

Correct nine more mistakes in the story.

Challenger, Summerlee, Roxton and Malone travel into the Amazon by ~~train~~ boat. Gomez and Manuel – two men from Ecuador – go with them and they have four Indians and a strong man to help them. The strong man's name is Rambo. Challenger and the others see Indians all around them, but the Indians don't attack. Challenger's group follows the Amazon River for some time. Then when they see a strange, thin rock they leave the Amazon and follow a smaller river. In the end they leave this river and walk up a hill. Here they find four black bones and see something large and grey climbing into some trees. Then they find the cliffs of Maple White's drawing. Near the cliffs they find a dead woman. They can't take Maple White's way into the Lost World because there is a wall of trees which stops them.

WORD WORK

1 Use the words in the drum to complete the sentences.

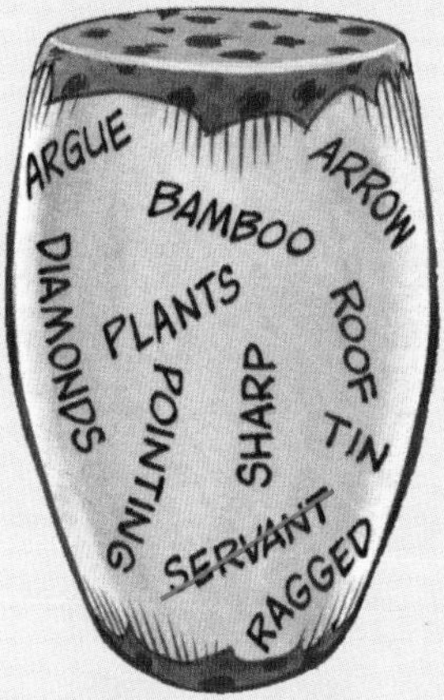

- **a** Zambo is a good, strong servant .
- **b** Summerlee and Challenger .... about a lot of things, but they agree that Illingworth is stupid.
- **c** The poor man was wearing old and .... clothes.
- **d** China has a lot of .... forests.
- **e** There are a lot of strange .... with beautiful flowers in the Amazon rainforest.
- **f** Don't touch that knife! It's very .... You could hurt yourself.
- **g** I don't like eating food that comes from a ....
- **h** Look at the strange bird in that tree – the one that I'm .... at.

i There's an .... there that shows the *WAY OUT*.

j When it rains, the water comes into my house. I need a new ....

k .... are very expensive stones.

2 Complete the words from Chapter 4 to match the picture.

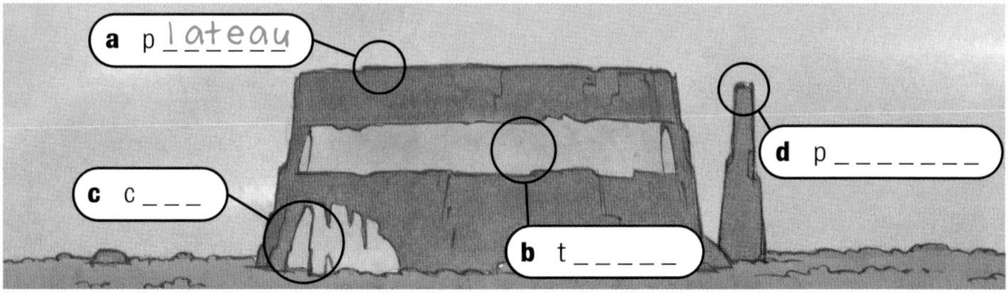

GUESS WHAT

What does Challenger's group do in the next chapter?
Tick one picture.

a catch a pterodactyl ☐

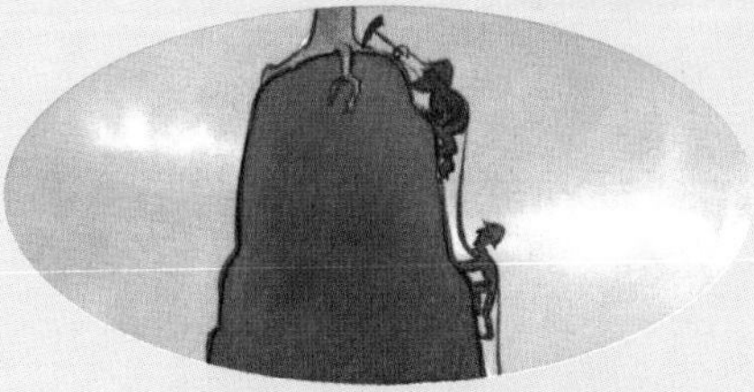

b climb up the pinnacle ☐

c break through the rock wall in Maple White's cave ☐

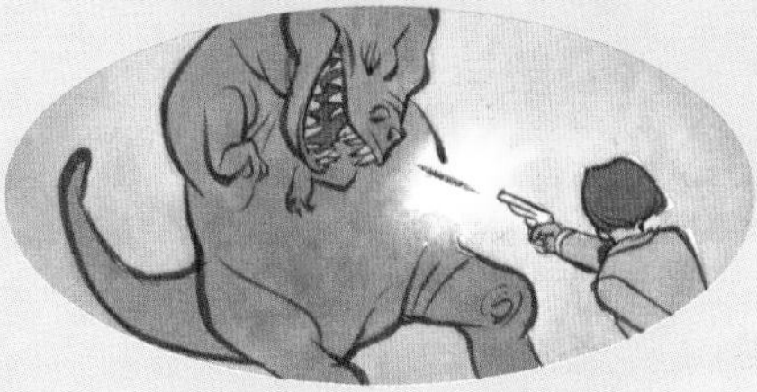

d kill a dinosaur ☐

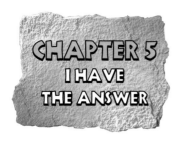

CHAPTER 5
I HAVE THE ANSWER

This was a wild, unfriendly place, and full of danger. But, when we looked up at that beautiful green plateau, we all wanted to discover its secrets and mystery. None of us was ready to go back to London yet.

Then, one night, something wonderful happened, something that changed everything for us. We were sitting around our campfire, and our dinner, a large chicken, was cooking on the fire. Suddenly, out of the dark sky, something flew down at us. We looked up and saw two enormous wings of grey skin, a long thin neck, a **horrible** red eye, and – to my great surprise – a hundred small, sharp teeth. A second later it was flying back into the night, with our dinner in its teeth.

For a long time, nobody could say a word. At last, Summerlee spoke in a quiet, shaking voice.

'Professor Challenger, I really am deeply sorry.'

Then the two scientists shook hands for the first time. The night the pterodactyl stole our dinner was truly a great night. The lost food didn't matter at all.

But we still could not get up to the plateau. After six days walking round the cliffs, we arrived back at our starting place, the rocky pinnacle. When I lay down to sleep that night, I could see Challenger sitting unhappily on a rock. His great head was in his hands, and he was thinking deeply.

But the next morning, Challenger was bright and smiling, and walking up and down **proudly**.

'I have the answer!' he said, holding his head high, and pointing to the pinnacle of rock.

We could see that climbing the pinnacle was not impossible. But what then?

horrible you say that something is horrible when you really don't like it

proudly in a way that shows you feel special or important

'Let us get to the top first,' the Professor went on, in a loud, important voice. 'There, G. E. Challenger will show you his plan.'

Challenger was a fine mountaineer, and with the help of a strong, fifty-metre **rope**, he climbed the pinnacle easily. After about an hour, the four of us were all at the top, together with Gomez and Manuel. From that high place, I could see everything — the rocky open ground below the cliffs, the yellow wall of bamboo, then the great dark green forest which went on for two thousand miles. It was a beautiful **sight**. I felt Challenger's heavy hand on my arm.

'This way, my young friend,' he said. 'Never look back.'

My eyes turned to the plateau. Its **edge** was perhaps twelve metres away from where we stood. So near, but still so far. I looked down, and saw our servants on the ground, far below us.

Professor Summerlee was looking carefully at the pinnacle's one great tree.

'This is interesting,' he said. 'It's just like an English tree.'

'It is,' replied Challenger. 'It's a friend from home in a strange country. And, believe me, that tree will be our friend.'

'That's it!' shouted Lord John. 'A bridge!'

'Yes, my good sirs, a bridge!' said Challenger.

It really was a very clever idea. It was my job, as the youngest and strongest man, to cut the twenty-metre tree. Challenger gave me the **axe** and told me where to make each careful cut. After nearly an hour of work with the axe, the great tree fell. One end of it lay at our feet, and the other end lay on the plateau. Without a word, we each shook hands with Challenger.

Challenger himself crossed the bridge first. Summerlee followed him, I went next, and then Lord John. So, at last, the four of us were standing in the lost world of Maple White. We walked a short way into the trees, then suddenly

rope a very thick, strong string

sight something that you see

edge the part along the side of something

axe you use this to cut wood

we heard a loud crash. We all turned and ran back to the edge of the plateau. The bridge was no longer there!

I looked down, and far below I could see our tree lying on the ground, broken into pieces. Then we looked across at the pinnacle. There we saw Gomez. His face was wild and strange, and his black eyes burned like fires.

'Lord John Roxton!' he shouted.

'Here I am!' Lord John called back.

'Yes, and there you'll stay!' screamed Gomez, with a loud, horrible laugh. 'We nearly killed you with that stone at the cave, but this is better. It is slower and more terrible. The hot sun will whiten your bones, and nobody will find them. When you are dying up there, think of Pedro Lopez. You shot him three years ago on the Putomayo River. I am his brother! Remember him!'

Then he and Manuel climbed down the pinnacle, and left us.

Lord John sat down on the ground, with a face like grey stone.

'It's my **fault**. You're all in this trouble because I killed Gomez's brother. I've been so stupid. Why didn't I think?'

We looked over to the pinnacle and saw that our good servant Zambo was climbing up as fast as he could.

'What shall I do now, sirs?' he called to us when he was at the top. 'The Indians are leaving, but I won't go, sirs, I'll stay with you.'

We told Zambo to throw one end of the rope to us. Then he **tied** a bag to the other end of the rope, and we pulled it across. We did this many times, and when evening came, we had food, water, guns, and everything for a clifftop camp.

That night I wrote a long letter to McArdle. The Indians were going home to Manaos the next day, and they could take it with them. Was it perhaps my last letter, then? There was no way to get down from the plateau. It was impossible. So I sat and wrote, in the bright, cold moonlight of this strange world, and I felt that there was no hope for us, really no hope.

fault when it's because of you that something bad happens

tie to keep something in place with string or rope

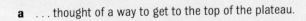

READING CHECK

Match the people with the sentences.

a . . . thought of a way to get to the top of the plateau.

b . . . saw a pterodactyl and said sorry to Challenger.

c . . . climbed up the pinnacle with the professors, Roxton and Malone.

d . . . cut down the tree at the top of the pinnacle to make a bridge.

e . . . crossed the bridge first and Roxton, Malone and Summerlee followed.

f . . . pushed the tree bridge off the pinnacle.

g . . . killed Gomez's brother many years before.

h . . . left Roxton to die on the plateau with the professors and Malone.

i . . . climbed up the pinnacle and sent food, water and guns across to the others.

j . . . wrote a long letter to McArdle.

WORD WORK

Use these words to complete the sentences.

horrible ~~proudly~~ sight edge axe fault rope

a Challenger told the others about his idea very proudly.

b I think that velociraptors were .... dinosaurs.

c Malone cut down the tree with a big ....

d Zambo used a long .... to send things across to the others.

e Malone stood on the .... of the pinnacle and looked down at the forest far below.

f Night changing to morning in the Amazon forest is a wonderful ....

g Roxton thinks that it's his .... that Gomez is angry with him and wants to kill him.

GUESS WHAT

What happens in the next chapter? Tick the boxes.

1 The professors are happy because they see . . .

a ☐ . . . a family of plant-eating dinosaurs.

b ☐ . . . a family of meat-eating dinosaurs.

c ☐ . . . a meat-eating dinosaur attacking a plant-eating dinosaur.

2 During the day Malone . . .

a ☐ . . . finds a way to leave the plateau.

b ☐ . . . climbs a tree to see all of the plateau.

c ☐ . . . discovers a lake in the middle of the plateau.

3 At night Malone . . .

a ☐ . . . goes for a walk.

b ☐ . . . runs from a meat-eating dinosaur.

c ☐ . . . meets a beautiful Indian woman in the forest.

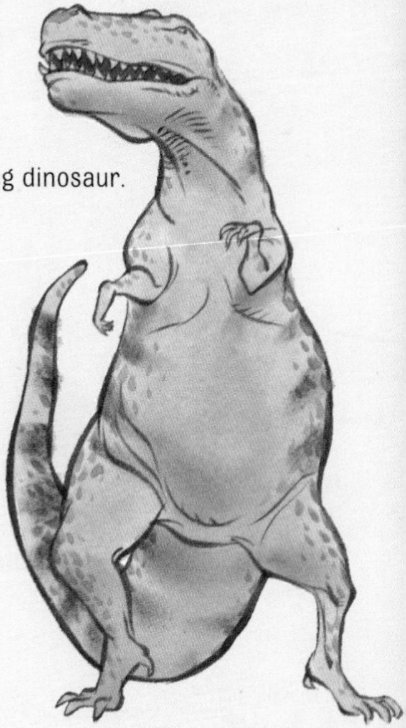

CHAPTER 6
A TRULY WONDERFUL SIGHT

'What shall we call this place?' asked Lord John, after breakfast.

'It can only have one name – the name of the man who discovered it. This is Maple White Land,' said Challenger.

We all agreed. We made our camp as safe as possible, building a wall of sharp plants around it. Then we began our first journey into Maple White Land.

The plateau was full of unusual things. Our scientists discovered many interesting plants and flowers. Late that first morning, we found some great **footprints** in the earth and followed them excitedly. Then, between the trees, we saw a truly wonderful sight – a family of five enormous grey-green dinosaurs. They were nearly seven metres long. We watched them from behind the trees, while they slowly ate great mouthfuls of plants. After a long while, they moved slowly into the forest. The professors looked **joyful**.

'What were they?' asked Lord John.

'Iguanodons,' answered Summerlee. 'Millions of years ago, England was full of iguanodons. Then they died. But here on this plateau, they are still alive.'

After about five kilometres we came to a large group of rocks. We heard some strange sounds, and quietly and carefully we looked over the rocks. The place was full of pterodactyls. There were thousands of the things sitting around little lakes of **stagnant** water. The smell was terrible.

Then they saw us. One after the other, they sailed up into the sky and flew around us in a large ring. Suddenly they attacked. A great grey wing knocked Challenger to the ground, and I felt sharp teeth on my neck. Another of the **monsters** flew at Summerlee, giving him a great, bloody cut across his face. Lord John pointed his rifle at the sky, shot, and a pterodactyl fell to the ground. The others flew

footprint a small hole like a foot that you leave in the ground when you walk

joyful very happy

stagnant dirty and not moving

monster a large and ugly animal

higher into the sky.

'Now!' shouted Lord John. 'Run for our lives!'

We escaped back to our camp, thinking that the day's adventures were at an end. But a surprise met us. Our things were lying all over the ground. One tin of meat was open, our cameras were **broken**, our box of **bullets** lay in pieces and there were bullets everywhere. But there was not a single footprint going to or from the camp.

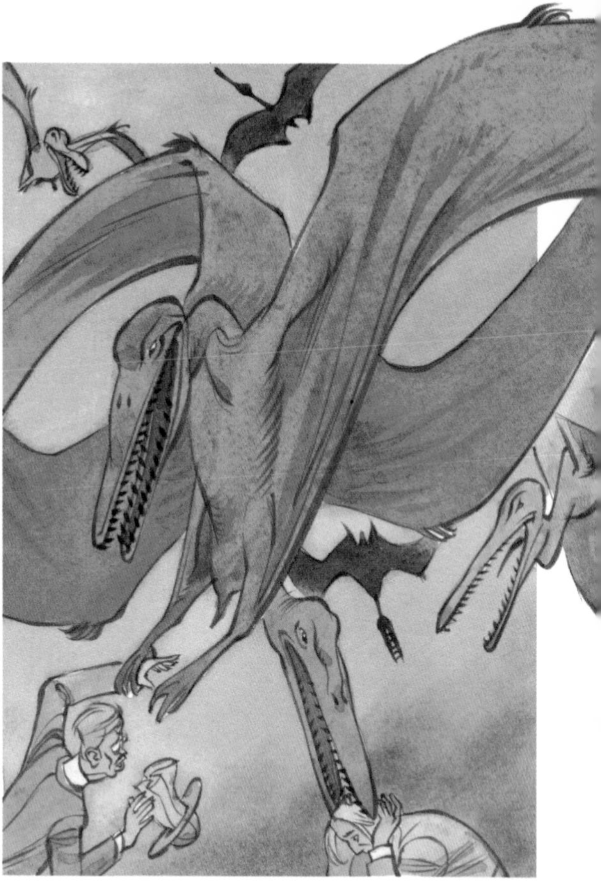

Perhaps someone or something used the large tree near our camp to cross over our high camp walls. At once I felt a deepening danger all around us. Whose eyes were watching us from those dark trees? What dangers were hiding in the silent forest?

That night I went to bed with my head full of these ideas. While I was lying there, Lord John asked me a strange question.

'I say, Malone. Remember the place where those flying things were? Well, do you remember the earth there, near the water?'

'Yes, I do,' I said. 'It was very soft – and blue.'

'That's right. Soft, blue earth . . .' he said, and walked away.

The next day we decided that we needed a **map** of Maple White Land. This time, I was the one who had the clever idea. There was an enormous tree beside our camp. Perhaps I could climb up it, and see more of the plateau. My friends

broken in pieces or not working

bullet a small piece of metal that you shoot from a gun or a rifle

map a picture that shows things like hills, lakes and rivers from above helped me to get up into the tree at once. I was high up in the great tree, when suddenly, I saw something – a face was looking into my face. It was long and thin, with strange, glassy grey eyes, and great sharp teeth. It was the face of an **ape-man**. For a second I saw a red hairy body jump through the trees, and then it **disappeared**.

For a minute, I could not move. But then I finished my climb, and soon I could see all of the plateau – forests, red rocks, and in the centre, a beautiful lake. On the other side of the lake were some tall cliffs, with dark holes in the side of them. Perhaps they were caves. In the soft evening sunlight, I drew a map of everything. Then I made my way back down the tree, and told the others about my meeting with the ape-man.

Later we put names on the map.

'What shall we call this lake?' asked Challenger. 'You saw it first, young friend, so you must give it a name. Lake Malone, if you like.'

'Well,' I said, **blushing**. 'I'd like to call it Lake Gladys.'

That night, the moon was bright, and I could not sleep. I got up, and quietly left the camp. I'll never forget that dark, lonely walk through the silent forest. After some hours, I saw water between the trees. Lake Gladys – my Lake Gladys – lay in front of me, silver and beautiful in the bright moonlight.

On the other side of the lake, I could see the tall cliffs again, with their round dark holes. But now there was something inside the caves – something bright, red, and burning. Fires! So there were men living on the plateau! I could even see the campfires darken for a second or two, when people walked in front of them.

I lay there for a long time, watching those red fires. Animals came to drink, strange and beautiful animals. Then came a great dinosaur, with a small head, short legs, a horrible blue-grey body and big sharp plates along its back. 'Where have I seen that monster before?' I thought. Then I remembered

ape-man something half-way between an animal and a man

disappear to go away suddenly

blush to become red in the face because you are shy or embarrassed

– it was the dinosaur from Maple White's drawing.

At half past two, I began my journey back through the dark forest. When I was about half-way back to the camp, I heard a long, deep **growl** behind me.

I walked faster, and the sound became louder and closer. Something was following me. My skin grew cold. I turned round, and suddenly I saw it – an enormous dinosaur, standing more than twelve metres tall. It gave a loud roar, and I saw its enormous sharp teeth, and the red blood around its horrible mouth. This was a meat-eating dinosaur, one of the most terrible monsters that has ever lived.

I turned and ran. But the monster's great legs carried it nearer and nearer to me, and its roar became louder and louder. I ran and ran, faster than I have ever run in my life. I felt its hot body close behind me. Then there was a sudden crash. I was falling, down, down, into something deep and dark.

When I opened my eyes again, all was quiet. Above me I could see bright stars, in a circle of black sky. I was in a deep hole. In the centre of the hole stood a tall stick, as sharp as a knife, and red with blood. This was a **trap**, made by the people of the plateau. A heavy animal that fell into it could never climb out again. But for a man it was not difficult. Before long I was at the top, looking out and listening. The dinosaur was far away by now.

The sky was already beginning to whiten, and I felt the cold wind of morning on my face as I went on home. But another surprise was waiting for me there. The camp was empty. Our things lay broken on the ground, and there was blood on the grass. I ran around wildly, calling my friends' names, but no answer came. All that day I waited for them. I could see our good servant Zambo, sitting by his campfire far below, at the bottom of the cliffs. But up here on the plateau I was alone. At last I fell asleep, thinking about my three brave friends. I have never felt so afraid or so lonely.

growl the deep noise of an angry animal

trap a thing that you use for catching animals

READING CHECK

Tick the boxes.

1 The professors are very happy to see the . . .

a ✓

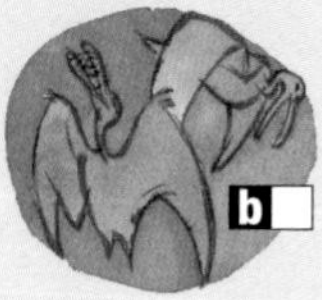

b

2

a

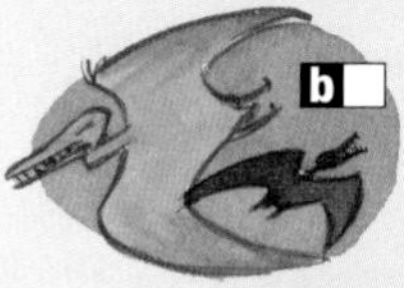

b

. . . attack Challenger's group.

3 Malone climbs a tall . . . to look at the whole plateau.

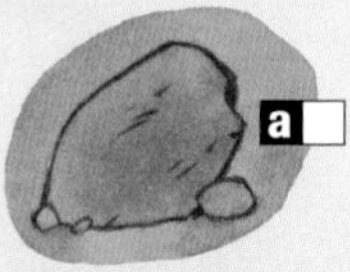

a

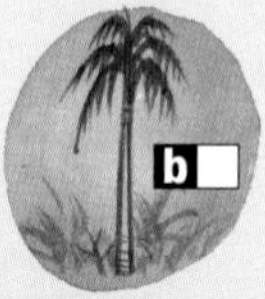

b

4 Malone runs from a . . .

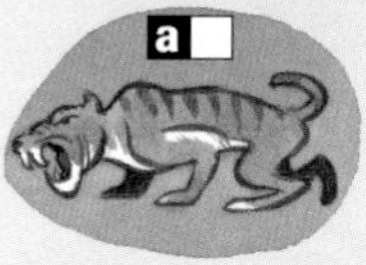

a

b

WORD WORK

1 Match the pictures with the words in the lake.

a footprints

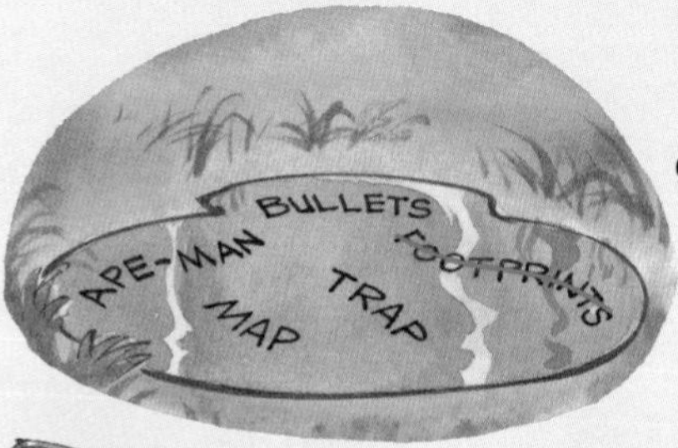

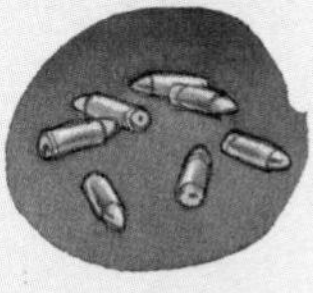

e ....

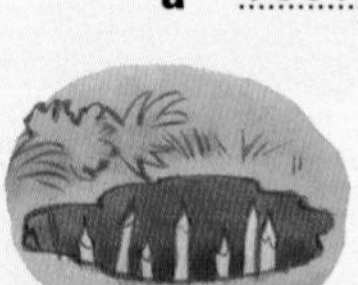

b ....

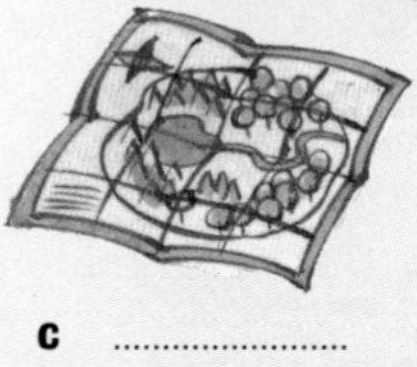

c ....

d ....

2 Find words in the leaves to complete the sentences.

a The professors are j o y f u l when they see the iguanadons.

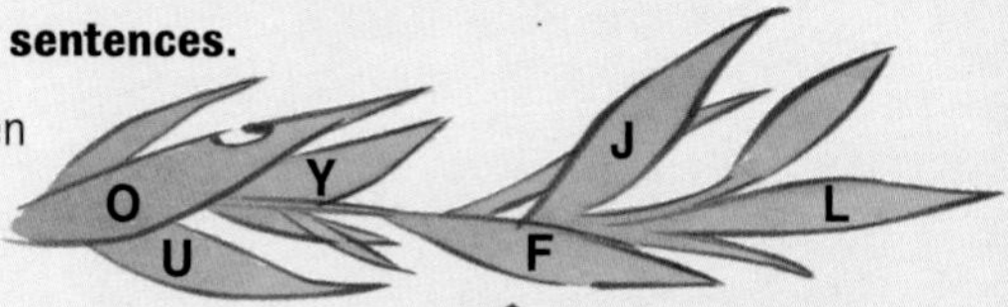

b Malone b _ _ _ _ _ _ when he names the lake which he finds *Lake Gladys*.

c There are b _ _ _ _ _ tins all over the ground in their camp too.

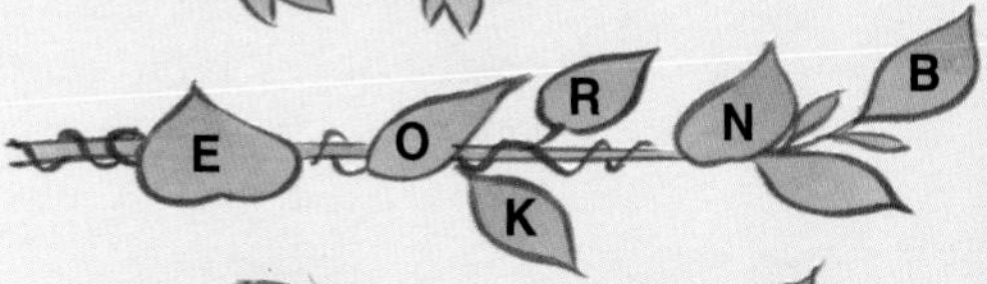

d The Hydra was a famous Greek m _ _ _ _ _ _ with lots of heads.

e When he is walking in the forest, Malone hears a g _ _ _ _ behind him.

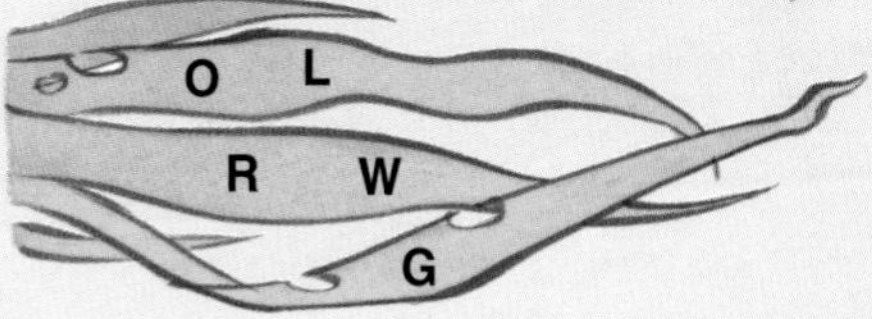

GUESS WHAT

What happens in the next chapter? Tick the boxes.

		yes	perhaps	no
a	Malone wakes up late the next day.	☐	☐	☐
b	Roxton comes back to the camp to get help.	☐	☐	☐
c	Challenger and Summerlee are with the ape-men of the plateau.	☐	☐	☐
d	Challenger and Summerlee are with the Indians of the plateau.	☐	☐	☐
e	Challenger and Summerlee die before Roxton and Malone can help them.	☐	☐	☐
f	Roxton and Malone save Challenger and Summerlee.	☐	☐	☐
g	Challenger's group helps the Indians to fight the ape-men.	☐	☐	☐
h	Challenger's group helps the ape-men to fight the Indians.	☐	☐	☐

CHAPTER 7
WE MUST MOVE, AND MOVE QUICKLY

The next morning I felt somebody touch my arm and my hand went to my gun. Then I opened my eyes, and I saw Lord John on his **knees** at my side. His clothes were ragged and dirty, his thin face was **scratched** and bloody, and his eyes were wild.

'Quick, young friend!' he shouted. 'Get the rifles! Get some food! Now run!'

A minute later, Lord John and I were running through the forest, with a rifle under each arm, and our hands full of food. At last he pulled me to the ground.

'There!' he said. 'I think that we're safe here.'

'What's happened?' I asked. 'Where are the professors?'

'The ape-men got us! It was early in the morning. They jumped out of the trees on to us. They look like animals, but they talk in a strange language, and fight with sticks and stones. They're as big as men, but stronger.'

While Lord John was telling me this, he was looking quickly from left to right all the time, with his gun ready in his hand.

'They took us to their town, **dragging** us along like animals,' he said. 'When we got there, they tied us up, and kept us as prisoners. But what about you?'

I told him about my adventures in the night.

'You say you saw caves,' he went on. 'Well, we've seen the Indians who live there. From what Challenger says they clearly found their way up from the forest floor to the plateau much later than the ape-men. They live on that side of the plateau, the ape-men live on this side, and there's a bloody **war** between them. Yesterday the ape-men caught twelve of these Indians, and brought them back as prisoners.

'Now, do you remember that forest of sharp bamboo sticks? Well, it's just under Ape-town, and that's the jumping-off place for their prisoners. One by one, the **line** of Indians

knee the middle of your leg; you move it when you sit or walk

scratched with thin cuts

drag to pull along the ground

war fighting between countries or people

line people standing one behind the other

had to jump off the cliff, while everyone watched. The bamboo went through those poor men like knives. It was horrible. Well, I was sure that we were next. But they decided to keep us, together with six of the Indians, until today. I escaped this morning by **kicking** my **guard** in the stomach, and I ran back to the camp to get the rifles.'

Just then we heard strange noises coming near us.

'Ssh! Here they come!'

I looked through the trees and saw the ape-men. They walked one behind the other, with short legs, great round backs, and long arms which touched the ground. I took my gun.

'No, not here,' said Lord John. 'We'll have better luck on open ground, where they can't run as fast as us. Let's wait a while.'

We had breakfast in our hiding-place, then began our slow and careful walk through the forest. After about an hour, Lord John fell down behind some trees, pulling me down with him.

'We're here! I hope that we're not too late,' he said, very quietly.

I looked through the trees. I will never forget the sight which met my eyes. On open ground, near the edge of the cliff, there were about a hundred of the red, hairy ape-men. In front of them stood a line of prisoners – five Indians, and two white men – Challenger and Summerlee.

Then the **chief** of the ape-men held up his hand. Two large ape-men caught an Indian by his leg and arm, and threw him over the edge of the cliff. The ape-men then all ran to the edge, and watched the poor Indian fall to a horrible death. They all laughed and screamed with joy, then waited for the next man.

This time it was Summerlee. The two ape-men pulled his tall, thin body to the edge of the cliff. Challenger turned to the chief, moving his arms about wildly. The chief pushed

kick to hit with your feet

guard a man who stops prisoners from running away

chief the most important person in a group

deadly killing

Challenger away, and held up his hand. But then there was a loud crash from Lord John's rifle, and the chief fell to the ground. He was dead.

'Shoot at them!' shouted Lord John. 'Shoot, my boy, shoot!'

We shot and shot, again and again. The ape-men ran around wildly. They could not understand where this **deadly** rain was falling from. Then, all at once, they left their prisoners, and escaped into the trees.

Challenger and I took poor Summerlee, and ran with him. Lord John ran behind us, shooting at the ape-men who were jumping down at us from the trees. They followed us, screaming, for more than a mile. Then the noise stopped, and when we arrived at our camp, we saw that we were alone.

But we were not alone for long. A minute later there was a soft crying sound outside the walls of our camp. We looked out and saw the four Indians from the cliff edge. They ran to us, and threw themselves at Lord John's feet.

'Get up, little men, get up,' said Lord John. 'Dear me, what can we do with these little **fellows**?'

'We need to take them home, of course,' said Challenger.

Far away, we heard the sound of ape-men's excited voices.

'We must move, and move quickly!' said Lord John.

Half an hour later, we were all at our hiding-place in the forest. There we rested our tired bodies. We were sure that the ape-men would not find us there, and the Indians soon became less afraid. They were small, with soft red skin, and friendly faces. One of them, a proud young man called Maretas, was clearly their chief.

The next day we sent one of the Indians to get water, but he did not come back for a long time. I walked a little way into the forest to look for him, and then saw something lying on the ground. It was the body of the Indian. I just had time to call my friends, before two long hairy arms came down from the trees. Two strong hands closed around my neck, and pulled my head back. I saw a pair of wild, glassy eyes, and a mouth full of long, sharp teeth. The hands pulled harder on my neck. There was a ringing in my ears, and stars danced in front of my eyes. I heard the sound of a rifle, and then everything went black.

When I woke, I was in our hiding place, and Lord John was giving me water. Challenger and Summerlee stood behind him, looking worried.

'We nearly lost you there, young friend,' said Lord John.

We now knew that the ape-men were all around us, watching our every move. Early that afternoon we left our hiding-place. The horrible cries of the ape-men rang in the trees behind us. Our fine young Indian chief walked in front,

fellow man

next came the other two Indians, and last came four very tired, dirty, and untidy white men.

We reached the lake in the late afternoon. It was a fine sight. A hundred small boats were sailing across the lake's glassy water to meet us. The men in the boats shouted with joy when they saw their young chief. They arrived on the beach, and threw themselves joyfully at his feet.

Maretas's father, the old chief, arrived wearing a beautiful animal skin. Maretas pointed at us and said a few words to his father. The chief shook our hands, then all the Indians fell down at our feet. I felt very uncomfortable at this, and I could see that Summerlee and Lord John felt the same. But Challenger loved it.

'Ah yes,' he said, looking down at them with a proud smile. 'These people know an important man when they see one.'

It was clear that the Indians were ready for war. Each man had arrows, and a bamboo with a sharp bone at the end. They sat down in a circle and began to talk.

'Well,' said Lord John. 'I'm going to go with our friends here, and fight those ape-men. What about you?'

I agreed at once. Challenger, too, was ready to fight. And in the end even Summerlee said that he would come with us.

Early next morning, four or five hundred Indians came together to meet their enemy. We walked at their sides, with our guns ready.

We did not need to wait long. There was a wild, high screaming, and suddenly the ape-men ran out from the trees. With sharp sticks and stones, they ran to the centre of the Indian line. But with their large bodies and short legs, they could not move fast enough. Indian arrows shot them down, one after the other.

The fight then moved into the trees. Here the ape-men were more dangerous. They hid in the trees, threw down sharp stones, and jumped down on us with their great heavy bodies. It was a long, hard and bloody fight. But the Indians were cleverer and faster, and at last nearly all the ape-men lay dead. The ape-men who were still alive ran to the cliff edge. They looked back, and saw that the Indians were following them. And with one long, terrible scream, the last ape-men jumped to their deaths.

'This has been a great day in the story of this country,' said Challenger. 'The ape-people of the old world have disappeared, and the plateau now belongs to the new world – the world of men.'

READING CHECK

What do they say? Complete the sentences.

I'm ready to fight, too.

Shoot at the ape-men, my boy!

Who is going with me to help the Indians fight the ape-men?

These Indians know an important man when they see one!

I'll go!

They're in Ape-town.

Where are the Professors?

I'll go with the three of you.

Get the rifles and run!

Here we are! This is Ape-town.

The plateau now belongs to the world of men.

a Roxton says to Malone: 'Get the rifles and run!'

b Malone asks Roxton: '..'

c '..,' answers Roxton.

d '..,' says Roxton quietly when they get near the apes' camp.

e '..,' Roxton shouts at Malone.

f Challenger says proudly: '..'

g '..,' asks Roxton.

h '..' and '..,' say Malone and Challenger.

i '..,' says Summerlee in the end.

j '..,' says Challenger after all the fighting is finished.

WORD WORK

Find words in the forest snake to complete Professor Summerlee's diary.

February

The ape-men came in the night and **(a)** dragged *Professor Challenger, Lord Roxton and myself to their camp. On the way my face was badly* **(b)** .... *by the forest plants.*

When we got to Ape-town, their **(c)** .... *came to see us. He was a very proud* **(d)** .... *(Like Professor Challenger with red hair!) There were* **(e)** .... *everywhere to stop us from running away, and we had to stand in a long* **(f)** .... *with some Indians of the plateau. There is clearly a* **(g)** .... *between the ape-men and these Indians, with lots of fighting.*

Suddenly, Lord Roxton ran off. He came back to Ape-town later with Malone and some rifles, and in a **(h)** .... *rain of bullets many ape-men died, and Challenger and I, and the Indians, escaped.*

GUESS WHAT

What happens in the next chapter? Match the two parts of these sentences.

a Roxton . . .	draws a map of the caves.
b The Indian chief's son . . .	argue with Dr Illingworth at the Zoological Institute.
c Challenger and his group . . .	opens the box and a pterodactyl flies out.
d Summerlee and Challenger . . .	goes to visit the pterodactyls again.
e Malone and Zambo . . .	doesn't want to marry Malone in the end.
f Challenger . . .	all leave Maple White Land.
g Gladys . . .	bring a large box into the Zoological Institute.

CHAPTER 8
UP WITH THEM!

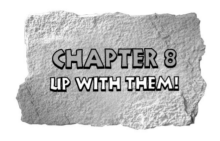

It was time for us to go home. The Indians were our friends, but they would not help us to leave. If we asked them, they just smiled and shook their heads. Only Maretas, the chief's son, looked at us sadly, and showed that he felt sorry for us. So we made our camp beside the lake, and tried to find a way to escape.

The lake was a wonderful place. The scientists joyfully studied all the strange and beautiful animals which lived in and around its clear waters. I did not know **exactly** why, but Lord John was very interested in some soft, blue earth at the lakeside. One day I met him wearing a strange round **cage**, made of bamboo.

'Where are you going like that?' I asked him.

'I'm going to see those pterodactyls. Interesting things, but not too friendly. That's why I'm wearing this. I'm also going to get a baby for Challenger,' he replied, and walked away.

Then one evening Maretas came to our camp, and gave me a piece of tree **bark**. He pointed to the caves above him, and put a finger to his mouth to show that this was a secret. Then he left. I took the bark to the firelight, and we all looked at it. It had black lines on it, one next to the other.

'What is it?' said Challenger. 'Writing?'

'I don't know,' I said. 'But I'm sure that it's something important.'

'I think that I've got it!' said Lord John. 'How many lines are there? Eighteen? And how many cave openings? Eighteen! I believe that it's a map of the caves!'

'He pointed up to the caves when he gave it to me,' I said.

'That's it, then!' said Lord John, excitedly. 'You see that **cross** here? That shows the cave which is deepest.'

'One that goes through to the other side!' I shouted.

At once, we went up the stone stairs to the cave mouths,

exactly really

cage an open box to put dangerous animals in, or to keep dangerous animals out

bark the hard skin that covers a tree

cross where two lines meet in the middle, like a '+' or 'X' being careful that nobody saw us. We found the cave, the second from the left, and ran into it. We followed the empty tunnel round to the right, but then we met a wall of rock. It was the end of the tunnel! But then I looked at the bark again, and suddenly I understood. The map showed a **fork** in the tunnel.

'I've got it!' I shouted, running back. 'Follow me!'

I was right. A little way back, there was a great black **opening** in the wall to our right. It was the longer arm of the tunnel. We ran down it, and we suddenly saw a bright light at the end. It was the moon!

'We're through, boys, we're through!' shouted Lord John.

We looked through the hole, and saw that we were perhaps thirty metres from the bottom of the cliffs. So we ran back to our camp, to get ready for our escape. One large square box, which belonged to Professor Challenger, gave us some trouble, but our other things were light and easy to carry. That night we secretly left the camp, and climbed quietly up the stone stairs. Just when we got to the entrance of the cave, we heard the strange, sad cry of an animal on the lake. Was it the voice of Maple White Land, saying goodbye? We turned, and went into the dark cave.

We soon arrived at the other end of the tunnel. Then, with the help of our fifty-metre rope, we climbed down off the cliffs. In the early morning we were at Zambo's camp, and a few weeks later we were on a ship, sailing home to England.

Our news went before us, and a large crowd of reporters met our ship when it arrived. But we did not say a word to them. We were saving our story for the meeting at the Zoological Institute the next evening.

The meeting was at eight o'clock, but the great room was full long before that time. Thousands of people were waiting for us, together with all the most famous scientists in Europe.

fork a place where one road becomes two roads

opening an open place

When we four arrived everyone stood up and cheered.

Professor Summerlee began to tell the crowd of our adventures. He spoke about our journey, but gave the listeners no idea about where the plateau was, or how anyone could get there. He talked about both the wonderful and the terrible things that we found in Maple White Land – the strange plants and animals, the iguanodons, the pterodactyls and other terrible dinosaurs, the Indians and the ape-men.

Then Dr Illingworth stood up from the crowd.

'A year ago Professor Challenger told us some unusual things. Today Professor Summerlee is telling us some even more surprising things. But that doesn't tell us that anything of what you say is true. How can we believe these stories?'

Some listeners shouted loudly at Dr Illingworth, others cheered.

Then Challenger got up, and argued with Illingworth for some time, while the crowd went on shouting and cheering.

'I have photographs of pterodactyls which will show you, without question, that—' began Challenger.

'Photographs are not enough,' said Illingworth.

'Then you need to see the real thing?' asked Challenger.

'Yes, I do,' replied Illingworth.

'And if I can show you the real thing, will you believe us?'

'Without question,' laughed Illingworth.

Then Challenger put up his hand. I knew what to do. I went out, and came back a few seconds later with Zambo, and a large square box. The crowd went quiet. Challenger took the top off the box, and out came a real, live pterodactyl. Someone screamed, and the pterodactyl opened its great wings, and began to fly in slow circles around the room. The smell was horrible. More people screamed, and the thing went wild, flying faster and faster.

'Close the window!' roared Challenger.

But it was too late. The pterodactyl pushed its great body

through the opening, and flew away into the night. Challenger fell back into his chair, with his head in his hands.

Then everyone jumped to their feet. A great crowd of cheering men were round the four of us.

'Up with them!' shouted a hundred voices. A second later they were carrying us along, high above everybody's heads. The crowd pushed out of the doors. I could not believe the sight which met us in the street. I heard a roar, and saw a hundred thousand people standing there. The crowds carried us along through the centre of London, shouting and cheering all the way. It was midnight when, at last, they put us down outside Lord John's home.

But what about Gladys? As soon as I could, I hurried to her home. I knocked excitedly on her door, heard her voice from inside, pushed past her surprised servant, and ran into the sitting room. She was sitting by the window. I flew across the room, and took both her hands in my hands.

'Gladys!' I said, joyfully. 'My Gladys!'

She looked at me, very surprised and pulled her hands away.

'Gladys! What is the matter?' I said. 'You are my Gladys, aren't you – little Gladys Hungerton?'

'No,' she replied. 'I am Gladys Potts. This is my husband.'

There was a small man with red hair, sitting in the corner in a soft chair – my soft chair. I found myself shaking hands with him.

'I'm sorry,' she said. 'But you went off to the other side of the world and left me. So I don't think that you ever loved me very deeply.'

I turned to the little man.

'Tell me something. How did you do it? What have you done in your life? Have you been on any adventures? Done anything dangerous? Discovered anything wonderful?'

'Well, no,' said the man. 'I've always worked in a bank.'

'Goodbye!' I said, and went off into the night, with a thousand different feelings burning inside me.

The next evening, my travelling friends and I all had dinner at Lord John's flat. After dinner, we sat together, smoking, and talking about our adventures. After a while, Lord John opened a cupboard, and took out a small box.

'Do you remember the place where the pterodactyls lived?' he said. 'Well, I saw something interesting there. It was a hole, full of soft blue earth. Now, I've only ever seen that once before – it was at the great De Beers Diamond **Mine** in Australia. So I spent a happy day down at the pterodactyls' place, and this is what I got.' He opened the box. Inside it were twenty or thirty brown stones.

'I didn't tell you about it at the time, because I wasn't sure. So yesterday I took one of them to the finest diamond-cutter in London.' He took from his pocket a beautiful bright diamond. 'And this is that stone now. He says that we'll get two hundred thousand pounds for this lot. That's fifty thousand pounds for each of us. Well, what will you do with your fifty thousand, Challenger?'

'I'll start my own **museum**. I have always wanted to do that,' answered the Professor.

'And you, Summerlee?'

'I'll stop teaching, and then I'll have time to write a book.'

'I'll use my fifty thousand to go back and visit the dear old plateau again,' said Lord John. 'And of course, you, young Malone, will use your money to get married.'

'Not just yet,' I said. 'I think, if you will have me, I'd like to go with you.'

Without a word, Lord John held out a strong, brown hand to me across the table.

mine a place where people get things out of the ground

museum a building where people can look at old things

READING CHECK

Correct the mistakes in these sentences.

a Roxton goes to catch a baby ~~iguanadon~~ pterodactyl for Challenger.

b Maretas gives them a map of the plateau.

c Challenger and his group leave Maple White land through the third cave from the left.

d They are on a ship going to England a few days later.

e Summerlee and Challenger tell everyone at the Zoological Institute that there are no dinosaurs alive in the world.

f Dr Illingworth wants to see a photograph of a pterodactyl, not a real one.

g Challenger's pterodactyl escapes though an open door.

h Gladys has married a man who is very adventurous.

i Roxton has brought back gold from the plateau.

j Challenger and Summerlee decide to visit the plateau again, Malone wants to write a book and Roxton wants to open a museum.

WORD WORK

Complete the crossword with words from the story.

1 The hard skin on the outside of a tree.
2 Place where one road becomes two roads.
3 An open place in a wall of rock.
4 People put dangerous animals in this.
5 People take diamonds or gold out of the ground here.
6 'He's about 2 metres tall.' 'About! How tall is he _ _ _ _ _ _ _?'
7 There are lots of old things for people to see in this building.
8 A 'x' or '+'.

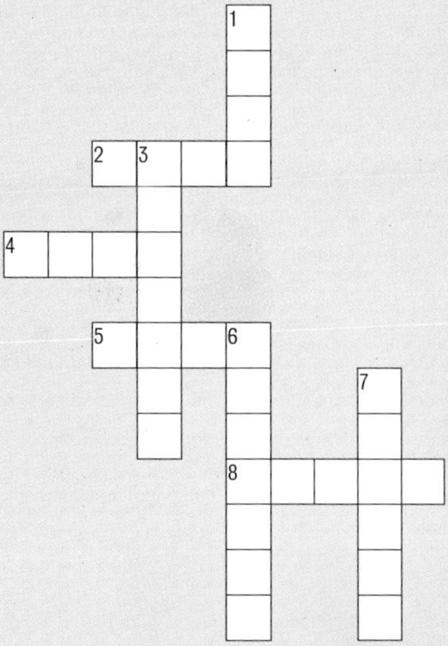

GUESS WHAT

What do you think happens after the end of the story? Choose from these ideas or add your own.

a ☐ Summerlee writes a book about dinosaurs and becomes very rich.
b ☐ Challenger opens a Dinosaur Museum and becomes very famous.
c ☐ Malone meets a beautiful Brazilian woman and marries her.
d ☐ Lord John starts a diamond mine and dinosaur park called *The Lost World*.
e ☐ Gladys gets bored in London and becomes an explorer.
f ☐ Dr Illingworth loses his job and everyone laughs at him.
g ☐ McArdle asks Malone to write about his adventures for the *Gazette*.
h ☐ ....
i ☐ ....

PROJECT A

A letter from Malone

1 **Read this letter from Edward Malone to Gladys Hungerton. When did he write it? Find the page in the story.**

43 Martin Square
London W3
18th November

Dear Gladys,

My adventure has begun. I went to a meeting at the Zoological Institute last night and listened to a talk about dinosaurs. Professor Challenger was there. I told you about him, remember? He says that he knows a place in South America where there are living dinosaurs. I am going to find this place with Challenger, Professor Summerlee and Lord John Roxton, the famous explorer.

I will write again soon, my darling.

Lots of love,
Edward

2 Write this letter again with the correct punctuation.

16 Ham Lane London W10 22nd November Dear Edward Thank you very much for your letter of the 18th November This adventure of yours to South America to find some living dinosaurs is a good idea my darling I'm sure that it will be very exciting for you Perhaps when you come home I will marry you I look forward to hearing from you again soon Lots of love Gladys

3 Write another letter from Malone to Gladys. Write about one of the places in the pictures.

The *Daily Gazette* offices

Professor Challenger's house

The Zoological Institute

Lord John's flat

On the ship

The Amazon

The red cliffs

The Lost World

PROJECT B

MY FAVOURITE DINOSAUR

1 Read the project and complete the table at the bottom of the page. Use a dictionary to help you.

ALL ABOUT MY FAVOURITE DINOSAUR

My favourite dinosaur is the Corythosaurus. It lived 75 million years ago. It was 10 metres long and it weighed 4 tonnes. It ate plants.

Corythosaurus lived in what is now North America.

I like Corythosaurus because it looks funny - like a duck - and because it was a plant-eating dinosaur. I don't like fierce meat-eating dinosaurs very much. It walked on its back legs.

Dinosaur name	
When it lived	...... million years ago
Length	...... metres
Weight	...... tonnes
Diet	
Where it lived (habitat)	
Why it's my favourite dinosaur	

2 Use the information in the table to complete the project about Gallimimus.

Dinosaur name	Gallimimus
When it lived	73 million years ago
Length	6 metres
Weight	225 kg
Diet	small animals and plants
Where it lived (habitat)	Asia
Why it's my favourite dinosaur	looks weird - like a chicken; ran on back legs

Gallimimus lived .... million years ago. It was .... metres long and it weighed .... It ate .... and ....

Gallimimus lived in what is now ....

I like Gallimimus because it looks .... - like a .... - and because it ate .... and .... Just like humans! It ran on its back legs.

3 Use the information on page 58 (or from your own research) to make a project about a dinosaur.

Triceratops

When it lived *67-65 million years ago*
Length *9 metres*
Weight *4.8 tonnes*
Diet *plants*
Where it lived (habitat) *what is now North America*
Why it's interesting *looks funny - like a rhinoceros with three horns; walked on all four legs*

Iguanadon

When it lived *140-110 million years ago*
Length *9 metres*
Weight *4 tonnes*
Diet *plants*
Where it lived (habitat) *what is now Europe*
Why it's interesting *had claws on its hands; walked on all four legs, sometimes on back legs*

Tyrannosaurus Rex

When it lived *68-65 million years ago*
Length *12 metres*
Weight *5.7 tonnes*
Diet *plant-eating dinosaurs*
Where it lived (habitat) *what is now North America*
Why it's interesting *looks frightening; walked on back legs*